From the Notebooks of Korah's Daughter

Linda Stern Zisquit

NEW WALK EDITIONS
Nottingham • Leicester

Acknowledgments

Grateful acknowledgment is made to the following publications where some of these poems originally appeared: *arc 24, Shirim, Salamander, Salmagundi,* and *PN Review.*

Thanks to the Hadassah-Brandeis Institute and the Memorial Foundation for Jewish Culture for grants that helped me while working on these poems.

978-1-9998026-7-7

Published by New Walk Editions
c/o Nick Everett, Centre for New Writing,
University of Leicester, LE1 7RH
and
c/o Rory Waterman,
Nottingham Creative Writing Hub,
Nottingham Trent University, NG11 8NS
www.newwalkmagazine.com

Printed by imprintdigital, Upton Pyne, Exeter.

Contents

...like a tree planted by rivers of water [Ps. 1]

Not to think moving to another
room will open the pores or seal
the sorrow. It seeps in because
you are the keeper who lets it in.
No door wide open or shut would have
let this happen. Clear from the start:
a tree, *yielding its fruit in season*.
At the bottom of steps a garden grows.
I could go outside and drink in
the green. For now I must keep myself
fixed to this chair, this text, this
fleeting existence. Was it yesterday
I thought they dug deep, cut the hole
clean to the root, not a cell left
to fester or seek an unseen crack,
then closed the wound to heal,
nothing withered. By chance today
I draw an image of before – the hair,
the mouth, the brow: a girl
emerging from the stream, urgent
yet uncertain, her fullness
smiling out at me.

Why do nations rage and people think only of vanities [Ps. 2]

Anxious to see him, how could it be otherwise!
Will he come from behind and scare off
the light? Or from in front where lifting my
face the light of his will shine? Is that his
whistle, or another's? Would I recognize
his step? We speak of a poet's tears
after years away from home: the island,
the quiet sea, the sun. Why exiled? For songs
in a foreign tongue! And why did I embrace him
on the street just as the elder walked by?
Was it in order to be banished, never to
see him again? The man in the long black robe
could not have seen us and smiled as he passed.
Still I took an oath not to endanger him again.
Not to allow the open windows and waiting faces
to condemn. If I leave of my own volition
I avoid the vanity and rage, the fiction of wisdom.

I lie down and sleep and wake [Ps. 3]

Even as I lie to your face. Even as I
pursue the wrong path. Blot out
my mistakes and nothing remains:
gaps and stolen music from between
the two pear trees. Even there
the fruit falls. Too soon it ripens
and I must gather the rotten,
the pungent, the worm-infested.
Yet this troubled sleep is balm
because it takes me and holds me
and does not question what I did
in daylight, now erased. What is
sleep? Sustain me. I no longer promise
to be good. And still sleep comes.
Or vow to be clean. No. The white
linen soiled, my sweat where flesh
desires more. I don't ask for
stillness or for stone, chiseled as
the stoic, the monk, the penitent.
Only for soft earth, its throbbing
mouth, fresh grass with its wetness,
the heart listening, awake now, alone.

For the musician on stringed instruments, answer when I call [Ps. 4]

We are hanging by a thread.
Rumors of more dead, rumors that
pass like a measure of song whispered
in ears: dead, your sons are dead.
How will I write the next line
or go out on a summer day to sing?
If you hear when I call to you why
don't you answer? It is demeaning
to think we are bound to a fate
that keeps taking our young.
Let them run with their mates
for two months to the hills,
to dance and lament the kisses
ungiven, like Yiftah's daughter
fulfilling a father's reckless vow,
as if this were the promise
that puts gladness in our hearts.

With an eight-stringed harp. In the grave who can give thanks? [Ps. 6]

I will try with my fingers to pluck
the chords to please you. Though I
have never been fully turned or
tuned to your mercy. As the demon
slips into my veins *I cause my bed*
to swim, out of desire for him,
not you. And not in grief, but
longing. It is my instrument,
the body's heat. And the wooden
bridge across which my bow plays
is taut. Still I am one of the lost,
my bones frightened not by a spear
or a soldier's bleeding arm
but in fear of nothing but this
pulsing lyre. With an eight-
stringed lark the skies explode.
With an eight-stringed heart
the body tenses and knows.
Keep me from silencing song.

What is man, that You keep him in mind [Ps. 8]

How easily we fall. The boy. The man.
The doomed daughter liberated
by death from the moon and stars
that you have pinned in place.
How is it they remain fixed
and you have let the boy loose,
the man unhinged from his home,
a stray jackal roaming the hills,
howling? What is the mind
in which you keep us unarmed
against your cosmos? No belief or creed
is strong enough to cry out: more.
Not even your name over the earth.

You have destroyed their cities; the memory of them is gone [Ps. 9]

Only names if we give them names
will call back what happened.
Even in our tongue, though they
spoke another. Even if *graves*
of desire are left open, the spoils
spread around, ravaged
as Tyre. Even if we recount
the journey from the death of their
first-born to Moab, to Canaan,
even if we track their steps
with a line across their land and
ours, it is only by naming them
that we can be forgiven, or forgive
ourselves who traverse the same route
spotted with nettles and revenge.

He has hidden His face; He will never see [Ps. 10]

Wherever I look, there you were meant
to be. In villages and towns, on the road
to the station, there you must be,
your shadow over everything. The acts
called evil are witnessed. But where
are the eyes and ears that will verify
these things? Like the perpetrator you
hide. The lion. The mocker. Is that
the work of a god, to join the pack
of those who lurk unseen?
On the agitated lane I meet friends,
comfort a child who is pressed
with the weight of your hiddenness,
with the moving force of war and
prophecy. With the inability to take a
breath amid the smoke, to breathe
as your presence nears, to recognize it.

How can you say to my soul, flee as a bird to your mountain? [Ps. 11]

Trembling in our cage of fear, our limbs too weak
to grip the bars: we are in the care of careless men.
A girl cries from an underground tunnel, not the terror

hole of bitumen and pitch, but a buried light that is poetry.
She sings a sharp trill. A man whistles in the orchard.
It took him hours to arrive from Beit Hanina, 'House of Pity'.

We shake hands amid the bulbul's noisy song as if to mark
a meeting ground. Her voice carries through a faint line, reaches
me with its human cry like a small bird's, a soul escaping.

How long must I devise plans in my soul, have sorrow in my heart all day? [Ps. 13]

A disordered mind turns in two
directions when she speaks these words:
toward skies filled with the noise
of new birds babbling, mimicking
their elders, testing and sounding
till they emit a call of their own;

and toward Sheol where she cannot
hear a wing's whir, now that he
who leaves is silent: as he crosses
the universe no echo over the earth,
as she recalls his tremor and knows
in his throat are movements and in
his limbs like feathers a fluttering.

...Who has counseled me, even on nights when my thoughts are tortured [Ps. 16]

Who has brought me to this mountain
surrounded by trees, looking out
on Lebanon after a day of intense
heat, serene as the stretch of grass
before the sanctuary walls? We climbed
ramparts, walked between pillars
and poles to a dusty shrine
within the pine-tree hedge of a village.
I have come to this refuge under
the good auspices of some god.
A soldier captured, two more dead.
My own battle goes on within.
He who has counseled me at night –
even when my thoughts are
tortured, when longing is more than
I can bear – has brought me here.

Guard me like the pupil of an eye; hide me in the shadow of Your wings [Ps. 17]

Wrens rehearse a local song, perch
in acacia native to this landscape.
There are patterns, chants
the birds learn before they claim
a call of their clan. I have unlearned
and discarded the elders' melody.
What I call seamless is the movement
from meeting him on a mountainside
and going home alone, the contour
of his body imprinted on my bare skin
that is never allowed to touch his.
Borders and wholeness are his
territory. Mine is lawless, broken.
Guard me like the pupil of an eye,
keep me within distance of sight, so
the shadow over my footsteps is called God.

He brought me out into open space; He rescued me because He delighted in me [Ps. 18]

We walked in the woods at dawn toward
an ancient red-bark tree when a pig-like
dog appeared on the path. It kept a few
paces behind as if assigned to us.
Once we cleared the rusty fence it took
the lead. Whenever we slowed down
because of loose rocks it went slower too,
entangling with our legs,
then racing ahead. Suddenly it stopped,
snarled and lunged at a thick snake
twisting and hissing from the branch above.
We spun round and ran, praying
it would show up breathless at our feet,
unsightly savior, angel of flight!
Entangled in the underbrush, how
do I sing of safety when I ache
to escape its wing? Like the ecstatic ones
who turned aside from your mountain
courting danger and mistake, I follow
every arrow leading me astray: where
is the hiss, the snarl to save me again?

…more desirable than gold [Ps. 19]

He spoke after love of honey.
The sun that shone behind him
blazed around us
though we were in shadow.
A bee dozed by.
If there is suffering there is also memory.
There is no utterance, there are no words
whose sound goes unheard:
speech of tree and whisper of stone.
I cannot forget the moment of his breath
or the light around his face,
a tree rustling,
pebbles stirring beneath us.
He said tomorrow and meant yesterday.
Gold becomes dim in the eyes
of the tired, the fire ceases to rage.
Only the sun still burns
with the glint of his gaze.

May He remember all your offerings. And accept your burnt sacrifice. [Ps. 20]

But nothing counts if we call it
victory. To be thankful is not enough
after war's obscenity: the feasts and
banners and rites and horns and drums
and shouts of joy. We grow dull,
haughty with relief, hardened to other
cries in the stony field. Or we awaken,
bend close to the ground, ear
to the grieving sand, heart humbled.

That I use the language of psalms
to sing of love, of honey in our mouths,
of his gold-rimmed face, is another
sacrilege. It is not enough to write
these words. Like the delicate spring
blossoms of the amaryllis I must
tough it out all summer, refrain from
easing away in the scent of his
robe. Not to forget your offering.

On Ayelet Hashahar. Gazelle of the Dawn [Ps. 22]

The cows and bulls surround me as we
hike up the hill to the temple ruins.
They follow me, strong bulls of Bashan
encircle me. *They open their mouths*
wide at me, like ravenous roaring lions.
Dogs snarl. Two roosters in a tree
at Bir'am tell of my wrongdoing. They
peck and stare as I count all my bones.
I have so many coverings, they divide
my garments among them and cast lots
for my clothing. The miraculous hand
of their god manipulates my regret.
Night brings no rest, I rub hyssop
for sleep, trace dogs and bulls and lions
retreating, fathom all the forms of
foreign love till I can taste the seed
of home, till my tongue does not cleave.

Who may stand in His holy place? He who has clean hands and a pure heart [Ps. 24]

I cleared the hours of the afternoon
to meet him in a cool tent. I washed
my body till it shone. I studied a treatise
to set the words of the wise on my tongue
before speaking with him. And he has
distanced himself from vanity and tired
of deception. He has a fortress to protect
from outside and in. He may stand
in the holy place with clean hands now.
I trip as I enter. Still it is half-open
to me, a door I could have closed
when first he appeared. Who can say
a heart is pure, pulsing its lonely poem?

At night one may weep, but joy comes in the morning [Ps. 30]

As though a sun rose inside us. Or
pulling ourselves up from the pit into light.
A scribe expresses desire, but displaced.
In stone. Or the beaten metal of a sunken
craft. It is through objects he can speak
of memory charged with forgetfulness.
Like a spirit-sailor tossed between
anchor and gale, torn between beauty
and the strict vows of a nazarite. To him
I embody division, our conversation
limned with coded hints of intimacy.
At night I weep, I try to sleep,
but joy comes in the morning. The way
the sea returns to shore, and expectations
rise in waves, carrying me out.

Malicious witnesses rise up; they ask of me things I do not know [Ps. 35]

Set judges at the gate, it is said,
and always at least two witnesses.
No crime exists if unseen:
things I do not know.
Like my secret in the field
where no witness came.
No one demands of me
justice or payment.
Only one whisper rises up
facing *Elul,* month of questions,
asking why did he lead me there
and why did I follow.
No one can prove I did not go
of my own will. No one can say
he kissed me or undid me
so I could not return from there
the same. Malicious witnesses
rise up within me. They propose
it was a crime I committed,
malicious witnesses who ask of me
things I do not know: tender as
the tissue of sex, tender as his tongue,
tender as the trap where we lay.

...in Your light we see light [Ps. 36]

We eat and drink and are sated.
The house abounds in your feast.
Is it hubris to speak of a
light-filled house?
A mother chants the word
summons
to see what is called to her:
a song she hums as shadows
flicker on a child's face.
You let us drink
from your spring
to quench our thirst,
brighten us with your gift.
The hole is dark and deep:
a silence of cries,
a barren hollow. Lift us
till we can bear your light.

What troubles you, sea, that you flee? [Ps. 114]

Is there a plan we cannot fathom?
The shawl she wore to veil her face
allowed the prudent man to know her.
The coat the brothers stained to hide their deed
betrayed their blood-tie to him.
The cloak she pulled from the servant's
beautiful back when he refused her and fled
remained in her hand as proof
of self-deception. We hide our tears
to protect a lie of recognition.
Recognize this! And a father understands
his beloved boy is torn apart
by a beast of his own conjuring.
What troubles you, sea, that you flee?
We are a moon tied to radiance
by a thread, we turn back and wait
to be thrust out, in turn, like the tide.

Rescue me [Ps. 140]

Snow falls covering the ground,
pressing down the branches, brightening
the night. We give thanks
for her recovery, your white clarity
around us, protecting.
Yesterday I met him at a well.
We spoke across the deep, never touching.
Rabbit in one language
could mean hunt or eat or brown
in translation. Asaph as a feminine
composer. Word-play before the second
sleep. These are the things we spoke of.
Not the tug and pull or even the music
that played silently between
us. Like a sudden snowfall at dusk.

NOTES

Each poem begins with a line from the Hebrew psalms.

> from *Midrash Tehillim*:
> The verse *But his delight is in the law of the Lord* (Ps. 1:2) applies to the sons of Korah, who composed a Psalm, saying: Are we still bound to honour our father [or] ought we to accord honour to Moses our teacher? Thereupon they decided in favour of honouring Moses.
>
> *And he shall be like a tree planted by the rivers of water* (Ps. 1:1). This verse, too, applies to the sons of Korah. After Korah and his company were swallowed up, Korah's sons remained standing like a boat's mast, as it is said, *They remained like a mast* (Num. 26:10). Rabbi said, 'All the area around them was rent, but the ground they stood upon was not rent.' R. Samuel bar Nahman explained that the three sons of Korah were not standing together in one place, but that each was by himself, so that after the earth was rent they stood like three pillars. Accordingly, in the popular saying, 'On what does the earth stand? On three pillars', the three are said by some to refer to Abraham, Isaac, and Jacob, by others to Hananiah, Mishael, and Azariah, and by still others to the three sons of Korah.

The English translations from the Bible are based on the *JPS Hebrew-English Tanakh*, the *New American Standard Bible*, the *King James Version*, and Machon Mamre's *Hebrew-English Bible*.

a poet (p. 6): refers to Elisha ben Abuya, a Talmudic period rabbi and scholar who adopted a worldview considered heretical by the religious sages of his time; they continued to cite his brilliant teaching by referring to him as *Acher*, meaning 'other'. One theory about time in the Bible is that 'there is no early and no late'; therefore, Korah's daughter might have had knowledge of the future Elisha ben Abuya, who would have appealed to her as a rebellious poet. A **poet** here also refers to Ovid, the Roman poet who, in exile in Tomis, yearned for his homeland.

Yiftah (p. 8) of Gilad appears in the Book of Judges. He led the Israelites in battle against Ammon and, after defeating the Ammonites, fulfilled a frivolous oath to sacrifice his daughter [Judges 11: 30-40].

graves of desire (p. 11): 'And the name of that place was called *Kibroth-hataavah,* because there they buried the people that lusted.' [Numbers 11:34]

Sheol (p. 14): underworld.

speech of tree and whisper of stone (p. 18): from an Ugaritic epic, *Ancient Near-Eastern Texts Relating to the Old Testament,* as cited in the *Jewish Study Bible* (Oxford University Press, 1999), p. 1303; according to the same source, an alternative meaning for 'their sound is not heard' is that the celestial bodies 'speak' soundlessly; they convey their message simply by being.

nazarite (p. 22): from *nazar,* literally, to separate; a nazarite is an ascetic who abstains from alcohol, does not cut his hair and is devoted to the service of God.

in the field (p. 23): 'For he found her in the field; the betrothed damsel cried, and there was none to save her.' [Deuteronomy 22:27]

Elul (p. 23): Hebrew month before the Days of Awe.

shawl, coat, cloak (p. 25): refer to the stories of Tamar and Yehuda [Genesis 38: 14], Joseph's brothers [Genesis 37: 31-32] and Potiphar's wife [Genesis 39: 12-14] who each used a piece of clothing for deception.

beast of his own conjuring (p. 25): refers to Jacob's state of mind when he sees the bloody coat and, knowing it is his son Joseph's, says 'an evil beast has devoured him, without doubt he is torn to pieces' טָרֹף טֹרַף [Genesis 37: 33]. Some interpretations find in Jacob unconscious fears and a sense of guilt and responsibility for Joseph's fate.